SPUNKY THE LITTLE HORSE

COUNTING SPUNKY'S FAVORITE THINGS

Melissa Ranney Weisser
Author

Grayson Stowe Weisser
Illustrator

© 2022 by Melissa Ranney Weisser. All rights reserved.

No part of this book may be reproduced in any written, electronic, recording, or photocopying without written permission of the publisher or author. The exception would be in the case of brief quotations embodied in the critical articles or reviews and pages where permission is specially granted by the publisher or author. For information regarding permission, write to melissa.weisser1@gmail.com.

Although every precaution has been taken to verify the accuracy of the information contained herein, the author and publisher assume no responsibility for any errors or omissions. No liability is assumed for damages that may result from the use of information contained within.

Publisher: Silver Arrow Barn Publishing
ISBN- 978-1-7364876-2-4

ACKNOWLEDGEMENTS

I want to thank everyone who supported me during the writing, editing and publishing of my book. Parker, Seth and Steve thank you for helping set-up for the photoshoot. Cowgirl Grayson thank you once again for all your design and computer help with "SPUNKY THE LITTLE HORSE "- Counting Spunky's Favorite Things book. My family is so amazing!

DEDICATION

While I was raising my three children; Madeline, Seth and Grayson, I always made teaching fun. We enjoyed learning to count by using objects or items they liked to play with. Madeline loved yellow rubber ducks and doggies. Seth was infatuated with yellow school buses, monster trucks, tractors and trains. Grayson adored her Breyer horses. This inspired me to create a book for counting objects that Spunky loves. Reminding myself, how fun it is to teach sweet little children to count. Special thank you to all the teachers in the world. You are super amazing. Happy Counting!

1
LEAN-TO SHED

SPUNKY goes inside his lean-to shed to protect himself from the blustery cold wind, beautiful white snowflakes, damp wet rain showers or the steamy hot yellow sun.

• Do you have a tree house or playhouse outside that you go inside for shelter?

2
MINI PONIES

Jazz is SPUNKY'S Best Friend Forever! They are together all the time. Inside the barn they share a stall where they sleep and eat. They really enjoy playing and chasing each other in the pasture. Jazz goes with SPUNKY when he is invited to Birthday and Holiday parties.

Do you have a best friend that you enjoy taking to new places and events?

3
JUMPS

You will find jumping classes at professional equestrian competitions. SPUNKY has a lot of energy and likes jumping for his exercise with Cowgirl Grayson. Exercise makes SPUNKY feel good and keeps him healthy.

- What is your favorite activity for exercise? Do you have a best friend you like to exercise with?

4
HALTERS

SPUNKY wears a halter when he is being led out of his horse stall, trailer or the pasture. Halters can be purchased in leather or nylon. They come in various patterns and colors. It is fitted around his nose, chin and over his ears. Cowgirl Grayson uses a nylon lead rope that is attached to the halter to lead him where she wants him to go. It is similar to a dog collar and a leash. It keeps Spunky from running off and obeying Cowgirl Grayson's commands.

Do you have a pet you like to take for a walk? Do you have a favorite color leash you use?

What color halter do you think SPUNKY would look best in?

Pick one of the following color's you like best.

5
BUCKETS

Buckets are used for holding grain, water, brushes, sponges, and bubble bath soap. Buckets are made in a variety of sizes (small, medium and large), and a variety of colors and material (silver metal, plastic or black rubber).

- Which color bucket would you choose for SPUNKY to use?
- Do you use a bucket to carry things from one place to another?

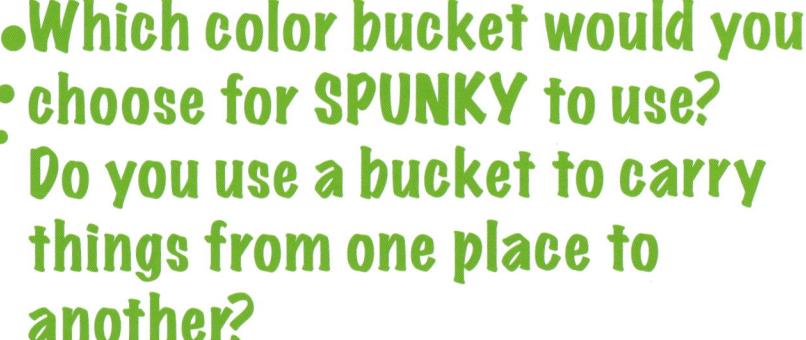

6
APPLES AND CARROTS

SPUNKY the little horse loves to eat fresh fruits and veggies. His favorite fruit is juicy red apples and his favorite vegetable is delicious orange carrots. SPUNKY loves the flavor of fruit and veggies, he thinks they are heavenly!

- Do you have a favorite fruit and vegetable you like to eat?
- Do you eat them as a snack?
- What colors are your favorite fruit and vegetables?

7
BRUSHES

Brushes come in a variety of colors, designs, sizes and textures. A brush either has soft or firm bristles. Softer brushes are usually used for everyday brushing and the firmer brushes are used to remove yucky mud and dirt. Cowgirl Grayson uses a firmer brush when she gives Spunky a bubble bath. He loves getting a bath when it is warm outside.

8 HORSESHOES

Horseshoes are used for working horses. For example, pulling a cart or plowing a field. Horseshoes are made of steel and shaped like the letter "U". They protect horses hoofs the same way shoes protect your feet. SPUNKY is not a working horse meaning he does not need horseshoes.

When you play outside what shoes do you wear? What color are they and how many pairs of shoes do you have?

Sneakers

Rain Boot

Crocs

Cowboy Boot

Sandal

Cowgirl Boot

9
HAY

Yummy for SPUNKY's tummy! SPUNKY the little horse loves hay like people love ice cream. Hay is green as a John Deere tractor and comes in a variety of flavors: pure alfalfa, alfalfa/grass mix and pure grass hay. SPUNKY and Jazz enjoy eating alfalfa/grass hay, they think it is the best. Good hay makes ponies fur coats soft and shiny. SPUNKY'S mane and tail grows thick and long. Have you noticed?

- What's your favorite ice cream?
- Do you eat it in a bowl or cone?
- Do you add fruit, flavored syrup or sprinkles?

10
TREATS

Horse donut treats are made with oats and molasses. These treats are extra fun because they have bright colorful sprinkles and icing. SPUNKY the little horse loves his donuts!

- What is your favorite donut?
- Do you like to pick out donuts that have icing and sprinkles?

A note from the Author

I grew up in Little Rock, Arkansas. I had my own big dream of living on a farm, and in 2000 that dream came true when I moved from Chicago to Indiana. I now live in Indiana with my husband, three children, farm animals and Spunky.

I wanted my children to live the American dream of fresh air, farm animals and a quaint community. My love for the country life and 4-H grows with every country breeze.

The 4-H Fair has been a large part of our family life. It has given the children the experience of loving and caring for their animals. Not only have they been involved with horses, they have participated in the swine, goat, rabbit, dairy cows, ducks and ceramics clubs. They had to select their 4-H Fair animals. Then they had the responsibility of feeding them, cleaning their pens, bathing and exercising them. It's a huge family undertaking but so rewarding. I encourage families to participate in their local 4-H Fair.

There are lots of great family projects (animals, crafts, baking, and much more).

I hope this educational book will make counting enjoyable for the entire family. Making special memories while teaching children can be a lot of family fun! Watching my children grow up, I realized the time spent together as a family is what you always treasure.

Spunky & Melissa

Other books in this series.

SPUNKY THE LITTLE HORSE
THE DREAM CATCHER

SPUNKY- his name says it all! For a little pony, he sure has some big dreams! Will Spunky's dreams come true?

Other books in this series, coming soon!

SPUNKY THE LITTLE HORSE
A CHAMPION?

SPUNKY goes to the 4-H County Fair. Will he win his very first event, the Western pleasure halter class?